UPHOLSTERY FABRICS

A GUIDE TO THEIR IDENTIFICATION AND SALES FEATURES

British Library Cataloguing-in-Publication Data
A catalogue record for this book is available from the
British Library

CONTENTS

A History of Upholstery

Upholstery is the work of providing furniture, especially seats, with padding, springs, webbing, and fabric or leather covers. The word *upholstery* comes from the Middle English word *upholder*, which referred to a tradesman who held up his goods, also connoting the *repairing* of furniture rather than creating new upholstered pieces from scratch. Traditional upholstery uses materials like coil springs (post-1850), animal hair (horse, hog and cow), coir (a natural fibre extracted from the husk of coconut), hessians (a woven fabric usually made from skin of the jute plant), linen scrims and wadding, etc.. It is done by hand, building each layer up in turn. In contrast, modern upholsterers employ synthetic materials like dacron and vinyl, serpentine springs, and so on. Today, the term is equally applicable to domestic, automobile, airplane and boat furniture. A person who works with upholstery is called an 'upholsterer'; an apprentice upholsterer is sometimes called an 'outsider' or 'trimmer'.

Traditional upholstery is a craft which evolved over centuries for padding and covering chairs, seats and sofas. Using a solid wood or webbed platform, it can involve the use of springs, lashings, stuffings of animal hair, grasses and coir, wools, hessians, scrims, bridle ties, stuffing ties, blind stitching, top stitching, flocks and wadding - all built up by hand. In the Middle Ages, domestic interiors were becoming more comfortable and upholstery was playing an important part in interior decoration. The decorations consisted mainly of what we would now consider as 'soft furnishings', though there were simple platforms of webbing, canvas or leather for stools, chairs and elaborately decorated coverings that already demonstrated the rudimentary beginnings of upholstered furniture.

By the beginning of the seventeenth century, chair seats were being padded, but this form of upholstery was still fairly basic. All sorts of stuffing from sawdust, grass, feathers, to deer, goat or horsehair were used, although in England the Livery Company forbade the use of goat and deer hair and imposed fines for misdemeanours. The stuffing was heaped on a wooden platform and held in place with a decorative top fabric and nails. This produced a simple dome shape sloping towards the seat. Only towards the end of the seventeenth century did upholsterers start to develop the techniques that would distribute and shape the stuffing into more controlled shapes. Curled horsehair was being used more consistently for stuffing, as it was easier to hold in place with stitches in twine (developed from saddlery techniques). Thus layers of stuffing could be distributed evenly and secured to stay in place. On a basic level, squab cushions were made more stable by using tufting ties. Stuffed edge rolls appeared on seat fronts providing support for cushions to be retained and later for deeper stuffing to be held in place under a fixed top cover.

In eighteenth century London, upholders frequently served as interior decorators responsible for all aspects of a room's decor. These individuals were members of the Worshipful Company of Upholders, whose traditional role, prior to the eighteenth century, was to provide upholstery and textiles and the fittings for funerals. In the great London furniture-making partnerships of the eighteenth century, a cabinet-maker usually paired with an upholder: Vile and Cobb, Ince and Mayhew, Chippendale and Rannie or Haig. What we now think of as 'classic' upholstery shapes and techniques really flourished in this century. Frames of elegant line and proportion were sympathetically matched by expertly executed upholstery. By now, the upholsterers' technical knowledge meant that stuffing could be controlled along upright and sloping lines, giving new levels of comfort and a simply stated elegance. Later in the century, the border was replaced by a single piece of linen or scrim (a very light textile, most commonly made from cotton or flax) taken over the stuffed seat and tacked to the frame.

In the Victorian era, fashions of opulence and comfort gave rise to excesses of stuffing and padding. Mass production techniques made upholstered furniture available in large quantity to all sections of society. The availability of better-quality steel springs and the development of lashing techniques enabled upholstery to be built up on seats, backs and arms quite independently of the frame shape. Stuffings became even more complex, edges became elaborately shaped into rolls and scrolls and fabrics were folded into soft padded shapes by means of buttoning.

Today, the practice and professionalisation of upholstery is very much an artisan craft. There are countless companies and individuals operating across the globe, providing uniquely crafted and highly sought after objects. Increasingly, hobbyists and those with an interest in DIY and home improvements are learning these techniques for their own constructions. We hope the reader enjoys this book.

A GUIDE FOR YOU

This booklet on furniture upholstery fabrics is printed to help you in your selling.

If you are a long-time furniture salesman you may find this little book a good source of information whenever you wish to refresh your memory.

If you are new in furniture selling, this book will help you to talk upholstery fabrics to your customers in an interesting and sales-effective way.

To make this information quick and clear, we took just the important highlights of fibers, weaves and tests—then compacted the briefed story into this handy pocket-size book.

We hope you find it helpful.

HOW FABRICS HELP SALES

To know upholstery fabrics is important to you because that's what your customers see first—see most of—and get the most lasting impression from.

So naturally your customers are keenly interested in the fabric's color, pattern, texture, durability, how easily it cleans and how comfortably it "sits". Women are particularly interested in these things, and they influence most of your sales.

So the better your knowledge of fabrics the better you'll "clinch" good sales, and build a profitable clientele.

KNOWING FABRICS IS EASY

Tne great variety of fabrics on furniture does not mean it's difficult to know them sufficiently well for sound selling. True—colors and patterns do seem unlimited, but actually there are only a *few basic weaves* and only *three basic types of fibers* in popular use today. Of course, extensive and most accurate knowledge of fabrics should come direct from the manufacturer himself. Requesting descriptive labels is one sure way of getting proper information. The tag shown on the opposite page is an example of a descriptive label that will help your selling.

6

But for your everyday help, this little book can keep giving you fundamental knowledge of the fibers and weaves now in popular use.

THREE THINGS MAKE THE DIFFERENCE IN FABRICS

1. The fibers or the blend of fibers used in weaving.

2. The type of weave.

3. Manufacturing skill and quality control.

WHAT FIBERS ARE USED—WHERE THEY COME FROM

Textile fibers are classified according to their origin—from animals or insects—grown in the fields—or made by man in the laboratory.

1. ANIMAL FIBERS—such as mohair from Angora goats, wool from sheep, silk from the silkworm.

2. VEGETABLE FIBERS—such as cotton, linen, ramie. All come from the soil.

3. SYNTHETIC FIBERS—man-made. They include various rayons, nylon and Aralac—the latter a new fiber made from casein.

Note: *Fibers* are the individual strands that make up the yarn that makes the cloth. *Fabric* is the cloth itself—composed of countless fibers.

WHAT DIFFERENT FIBERS LOOK LIKE MAGNIFIED

The character of an upholstery fabric depends a good deal on the fibers it's made of. Some use two or more fibers—some only one.

Since the fibers make a lot of difference in how well the finished fabric wears, feels and cleans—even though weaving is the same— let's look at the different fibers and see what's what.

TWO BASIC KINDS OF WOVEN UPHOLSTERY FABRICS—PILE FABRIC

Both pile and flat fabrics are woven—but there is this difference: Pile fabrics have a "pile" or surface of upright threads or third dimension, while flat fabrics are flat—no pile.

VELVETS and other PILE FABRICS come in different kinds—

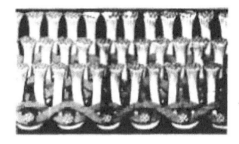

Plain Cut Pile Fabrics or Velvets have their soft pile starting up on end—thousands fibers in each square inch. Plain mohair is an example.

FLAT FABRICS—these have a flat surface. The yarns are interwoven at right angles—much like a handkerchief.

MOHAIR fibers are smooth, lustrous, cylindrical. An oil duct keeps them resilient. Dirt-resistant, durable and easy to clean.

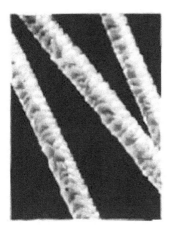

WOOL fibers are crinkly and have a scaly surface. They are durable.

RAYON and Synthetic fibers are smooth, sleek, lustrous. They resist dirt but vary greatly in durability and ease of cleaning.

COTTON fibers have a natural twist. They are soft and comfortable—but harder to keep clean because of absorbent qualities.

ND FLAT FABRICS

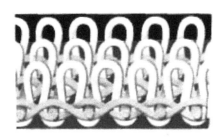

cut Frieze Velvets. This add of velvet has a surface of priads of tiny, uncut loops. They are available in many attractive patterns.

Cut-Uncut Frieze Velvets. Some of the fibers are cut as in plain velvet, others are looped as in frieze. It's a combination surface.

Jacquard Velvets are a special weave that permits intricate patterns. So Jacquard Velvet is patterned velvet with the pile either cut or uncut, or partly cut.

Claims, damasks, homespuns industries, and brocatelles are samples of "flat fabrics."

WHY SOME FABRICS WEAR BETTER

As you know, cloth in some suits wears better than in others. It's true of furniture upholstery fabrics too.

The fibers used, the type of weave, and how tightly the fabric is constructed can make all the difference in the world.

Fibers vary greatly in their durability. Fibers can be rated according to their abrasive strength but because of many uncontrollable factors such a rating is not always entirely accurate. However, if we rate the fabric fibers in order of their durability we find that, generally speaking, the order of durability is as follows:

Nylon, mohair, cotton, wool, viscose rayon, acetate rayon.

In weaves cut-pile fabrics or velvets wear best. Friezes also wear well because the surface loops are flexible and lessen the friction. Heavier and denser flat weaves give good wear.

WILL THE FABRICS FADE?

Your customers may voice this inquiry—but even if they don't you should be prepared to tell them if a fabric holds its color well.

What makes some fabrics fade and others resist fading? Well— the most important factors are the quality of the dyestuffs used and the thoroughness of the dyeing operation.

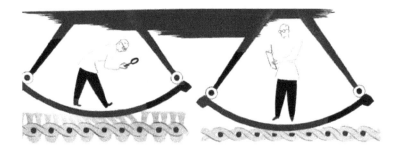

VELVET is the longest-wearing upholstery fabric because its fibers take wear on the *ends* or third dimension. As you see, this means a much deeper wearing surface.

FLAT FABRIC takes wear on the *sides* of the individual yarns. So generally speaking, these fabrics are not as durable as "pile" fabrics.

Please note, however: Unless the actual fabric construction is sound and properly balanced, even the best fibers and weaves will not wear their best. Loosely woven fabrics—where threads per inch are reduced to get low price—result in less durable material. So keep your eye out for good tight weaves.

Now neither you, your store, nor your customers can judge the color fastness of a fabric by its appearance. Few stores have the equipment to test fabric for fading. So you must depend on the reputation of a manufacturer for producing commercially fast colored fabrics.

This fade-test equipment, used by famous laboratories, tells in a short time whether or not a fabric is fade-resistant.

Of course no fabric is absolutely fade-proof—but there is a vast difference in the degree to which they resist fading.

The quality of the dyestuff being equal, the pastel shades tend to fade more quickly. Advise customers to place furniture away from direct sunlight.

WHICH FABRICS CLEAN EASILY—RESIST SOILING?

Your customers naturally are interested in getting upholstery fabrics that clean easily with materials at hand—and which also resist soiling and spotting.

Laboratory tests show that a fabric's ability to clean easily and keep clean depends a good deal on how it is woven and what yarns it is woven of.

Smooth-fibered fabrics like mohair—as pictured—are easiest to keep clean because they don't catch dirt so readily.

Velvet or pile fabric weaves, having a third dimension—as shown in the picture—break up the dirt before it can become embedded. Liquids too are broken up with less chance to saturate.

TELL CUSTOMERS ABOUT THIS MOTH GUARANTEE

Fabric manufacturers have done such a good job of moth-treating animal fibers that today retail furniture stores hear very few complaints.

Your customers, however, may like to have an even better guarantee than the assurance that the fabrics are "treated against moth damage".

So when you are showing furniture covered with Ca-Vel upholstery cloth, tell them this—

That all Ca-Vel upholstery fabrics are INSURED FOR FIVE YEARS against moth damage—insured without extra charge by one of the country's largest insurance companies.

This moth insurance not only covers replacement of the fabric, but *also cost of reupholstering.*

As you see—a smooth-fibered fabric with velvet weave has two qualifications. It tends to keep clean. It breaks up the dirt—making it easier to vacuum or brush away. And a good home cleaner generally removes stains.

Moreover, the furniture owner sends his claim direct to the insurance company with a consequent saving of time and costly service to the store. For your information, since the introduction of Collins & Aikman moth treatment, replacements have been a very small fraction of 1 %.

And by this guarantee both your customer and the store are protected.

LIKE *STERLING* ON SILVER

The National Bureau of Standards of the U. S. Department of Commerce has sponsored a commercial standard CS52-35 for mohair pile fabrics. This commercial standard is for the protection of the furniture manufacturer, the store, the furniture salesmen and for customers.

So by insisting on identifying tags, the furniture dealer and your customer can be sure that the fabric on the furniture you are showing either meets—or exceeds—government standards. Thus it will give satisfactory service.

When you display these tags to your customers tell them that the fabric is made by Collins & Aikman—one of the largest and most respected upholstery fabric manufacturers in America— the company that makes fine upholstery for America's finest motorcars, airplanes, buses, railroad streamliners, and modern steamships.

A FINAL WORD—TO YOU—TO YOUR STORE

As you know, there are *two* yardsticks of quality for upholstery fabrics—

1. One is by laboratory tests and what they show. (Only a *few* of the largest stores have this facility.)

2. The other is the long-time reputation of the fabric manufacturer. (And this quality gauge is available to *all* stores.)

Good merchandising and selling will help you trade-up your customers to the better grades of covers. As one example used by retail stores to effectively trade-up let's take a look at the Econometer. This simple but effective merchandising tool was developed by Collins & Aikman to convince the consumer that it is cheaper in the long run to buy the better quality upholstery fabrics.

Here's what it does. The wear tester tests fabrics for durability by measuring how much friction and rubbing they will stand. This "wear-ability" is one standard. The price of the fabric is the other.

By this means the store salesman can dramatically compare durability-for-the-dollar—a sound, sincere method by which your customers can often be traded up to genuine quality.

THE CARE AND CLEANING OF FURNITURE
UPHOLSTERY

Velvets and friezes may differ according to the types of fibers used in their makeup. The reaction of these fibers to cleaning solvents varies but the remedies mentioned in this booklet have been carefully selected and are applicable, regardless of the type of fiber used, provided instructions are followed.

General Instructions for the removal of stains from
automobile and furniture upholstery

1. Use clean cloths and a clean portion of the cloth throughout any operation.

2. Where the use of soap suds is required, use a neutral soap similar to Lux or Ivory.

3. Avoid the use of hot water, except where absolutely necessary.

4. As a cleaning solvent do not use gasoline which is colored or contains tetra-ethyl lead.

5. Do not use bleaches or reducing agents, inasmuch as their use tends to weaken the fabric and change or bleach the color of the goods.

6. Carbon tetrachloride is non-inflammable. Many other cleaning solvents are inflammable and care must be exercised in handling them.

7. Stains are more difficult to remove the longer they remain on a fabric. It is, therefore, advisable to remove a stain as soon as possible.

8. The direct application of cleaning solvents to the fabric, should, wherever possible, be avoided. Better success will be experienced by first applying the solvent to a clean cloth or brush, which is used for removing the spot from the area in question. There are exceptions to this rule, covered fully in the text.

In general no specific commercial cleaning fluids have been named. Those which are non-inflammable usually contain some chlorinated hydrocarbon such as carbon tetrachloride, together with various other hydrocarbons and organic solvents. Carbon tetrachloride is one of the best all-around solvents. The methods of treatment which are outlined have been tried out in Collins & Aikman Corporation's Laboratories, in comparison with many other methods described in standard references such as bulletins from the Bureau of Standards (U.S.), methods described in various textile handbooks and methods described by manufacturers of various cleaning fluids. Some of them have been developed in Collins &

Aikman Corporation's laboratories and in every case it is felt that the one described represents the best method available for treating the particular type of stain.

Instructions for Removal of Specific Types of Stains

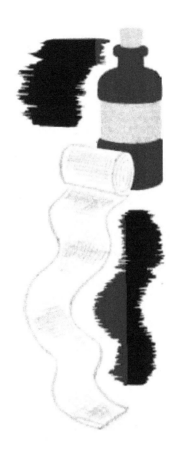

BLOOD

Rub the stain with a clean cloth wet with cold water until no more of the stain will come out. This treatment should remove all of the stain. If not, then apply a little household ammonia water to the stain by means of a cloth or brush. After a lapse of about one minute, continue to rub the stain with a clean cloth wet with cold water. If the stain still persists, the following method can be used: A thin paste of corn starch and cold water may be applied to the stained area. The paste is placed on the stain and allowed to remain there until dry. The dry starch is then picked off, removing the stain. Several brushings will then be necessary to remove the starch particles from the pile. For bad stains, several applications of starch paste will be necessary.

Hot water or soap and water *must not* be used on blood stains, as their use will set the stain, thereby making its removal practically impossible.

CANDY

Candy stains other than candy containing chocolate can be removed by rubbing with a cloth wet with warm water. If not completely removed, sponging the stain (after drying) with a cloth wet with carbon tetrachloride, will usually clear up the stain.

Candy stains resulting from cream and fruit-filled chocolates can be removed better by rubbing with a cloth soaked in lukewarm soapsuds, together with scraping while wet with a dull knife. Follow this by rubbing the spot with a cloth wet with cold water.

Stains resulting from chocolate or milk chocolate can be removed better by rubbing the stain with a cloth wet with lukewarm water. After the spot is dry it should be sponged with a cloth wet with carbon tetrachloride.

CHEWING GUM

Moisten the gum with carbon tetrachloride and work the gum off the fabric with a dull knife while still moist.

ENAMEL, PAINT & LACQUERS

If the stain is not dry, remove as much as possible by rubbing with a clean cloth wet with turpentine or the hereinafter mentioned solvent mixture. This may be the only treatment necessary. If not, then proceed with the method given for dry stains.

For *dry* stains—saturate with the following solvent mixture:

1 part denatured alcohol

1 part benzene

then work out as much of the paint as possible with a dull knife. After repeating the above treatment several times, saturate the stain with the paint remover solvent and immediately rub the spot vigorously with a clean cloth saturated with strong lukewarm soapsuds. Then subsequently rinse by sponging with a cloth wet with cold water.

FRUITS

Fruit stains of practically all kinds can be removed by treatment with warm water. Rub vigorously with a cloth wet with warm water. (If the stain is very old or intense, it may be necessary to pour a little warm water directly on the spot.) This treatment is not recommended for general use because some discoloration usually results from the direct application of warm water to such fabrics. If this treatment does not suffice, sponging after drying with a clean rag wet with carbon tetrachloride is the only further treatment recommended.

Soap and water are not recommended, as it will more than likely set the stain and thereby cause a permanent discoloration of greater magnitude, than the original stain. Drying the cloth by means of heat (such as by the use of an iron) is also not recommended for the same reason.

ICE CREAM

The same procedure is recommended for the removal of ice cream stains as that used in removing fruit stain.

If the stain is persistent, rubbing the spot with a cloth wet with warm soapsuds may be used to some advantage, after the initial treatment with hot water. The soapsuds should then be removed with a clean wet cloth. After drying, a sponging with carbon-tetrachloride will clean up the last traces of the stain, by removing the fatty or oily matter.

INK (Writing Ink)

The composition of writing inks varies: therefore, it is impossible to find agents which are equally effective in removing all ink spots. In general, no ink spot can be completely removed from velvets and flat fabrics without injuring the goods. The following methods are recommended and are listed according to their relative efficiency:

1. Commercial ink removers

A. Gartside's Iron Rust Soap, manufactured by the Gartside's Iron Rust Soap Co., Philadelphia, Pa. and on sale throughout the United States.

(Rub the soap into the stain with the fingers.) Let stand about a minute and wipe off with dry cloth. Repeat the process till the wiping cloth no longer shows a stain. Then rinse by rubbing the spot with a cloth wet with cold water.

B. Carter's Ink Eraser *No. 1* Solution manufactured by the Carter's Ink Co., Boston, Mass., and on sale at most all drug stores. Solution No. 2 cannot be used since it changes the color of fabrics.

(Apply No. 1 Solution to the spot with eye-dropper and then blot with blotting paper.) Repeat process until a clean portion of blotting paper shows no stain. Then rinse by rubbing with clean cloth wet with cold water.

2. Saturated solution of oxalic acid. This is a deadly poison, therefore it must be kept out of reach of children and away from the mouth. Use as outlined in 1, B.

3. 2% solution of Sodium acid Fluoride (Sodium bi-fluoride). Use as outlined in 1, B.

LIPSTICK

Apply a little carbon tetrachloride to the stain by means of a saturated cloth and immediately press a blotter firmly on the spot. Repeat this procedure, using new sections of blotting paper until the blotter no longer shows stain.

LIQUOR AND WINE

Treat liquor and wine stains in exactly the same manner as fruit stains.

SHOE POLISH AND DRESSINGS

Black and Tan—Rub the stain with a cloth wet with carbon tetrachloride until removed. Care must be taken so that a clean portion of the cloth is used for each rubbing operation.

White—Allow the polish to become dry. Then brush the spot vigorously with a brush. This will probably be all the treatment that is necessary. If not, then moisten the spot with cold water and after it has again dried repeat the brushing operation.

URINE

Sponge the stain with a clean cloth wet with lukewarm soapsuds and then rinse well by rubbing the stain with a clean cloth wet with cold water. Then apply to the spot, using a saturated cloth, a mixture composed of one part household ammonia water and five parts of water. Allow it to remain for a minute and then rinse by rubbing with a clean wet cloth.

Lightning Source UK Ltd.
Milton Keynes UK
UKHW010858060323
418095UK00001B/289